a special gift for

_____

with love,

_____

date

_____

Stories, sayings, and scriptures to Encourage and Inspire

hugs™

for
Granddaughters

CHRYS HOWARD
Personalized Scriptures by
LEANN WEISS

HOWARD
PUBLISHING CO.

This book is dedicated to my
five precious granddaughters,

*Sadie, Macy, Ally,
Aslyn, and Bella.*

I love you more
than words can express
and enjoy every minute
I share with you!
May the Lord bless you
and keep you safe.

Love, 2-Mama

Our purpose at Howard Publishing is to:

- *Increase faith* in the hearts of growing Christians
- *Inspire holiness* in the lives of believers
- *Instill hope* in the hearts of struggling people everywhere

Because He's coming again!

Hugs for Granddaughters © 2005 Chrys Howard
All rights reserved. Printed in the United States of America
Published by Howard Publishing Co., Inc.
3117 North 7th Street, West Monroe, LA 71291-2227
www.howardpublishing.com

05 06 07 08 09 10 11 12 13 14   10 9 8 7 6 5 4 3 2

Paraphrased scriptures © 2005 LeAnn Weiss, 3006 Brandywine Dr.
Orlando, FL 32806; 407-898-4410

Edited by Between the Lines
Interior design by Stephanie D. Walker
Photography by Chrys Howard

Library of Congress Cataloging-in-Publication Data
Howard, Chrys, 1953–
    Hugs for granddaughters : stories, sayings, and scriptures to encourage and inspire /
    Chrys Howard ; personalized scriptures by LeAnn Weiss.
        p. cm.
    ISBN: 1-58229-416-X
    1. Granddaughters—Religious life. 2. Grandparent and child—Religious
aspects—Christianity. I. Weiss, LeAnn. II. Title.

BV4571.3.H69 2005
242'.643—dc22

2004054125

Contents

*Grandchildren are the
dots that connect
the lines from generation
to generation.*

Lois Wyse

Making Life Fun

Chapter One

1

Enjoying life is a gift from Me to you. Let Me keep you occupied with a glad heart. Even before you were born, I thought countless precious thoughts of you and ordained all of your days. My love is always before you.

Smiling on you,
Your God of Life

—from Ecclesiastes 5:19–20; Psalms 139:16–17; 26:3

When you were born, your grandparents felt as though the world had stopped spinning. Busy schedules came to a sudden halt. Cameras flashed, tears flowed, and hands reached out to take their turn holding you. An actress making her debut on the red carpet wouldn't get more devoted attention than you did on your opening day! You were the center of their world.

Even today, the expression "wrapped around your little finger" doesn't begin to describe how important, how special, how much fun you are and always will be to your grandparents.

You see, somewhere along the way, before
you came along, life had distracted them from the
fun of picking a four-leaf clover or jumping into a
swimming pool or riding a bike with no hands. But
that's where a granddaughter comes in. You remind
them how much fun life can be.

There's more to it than just the activities you share
with them. Knowing how much you love them
makes life more enjoyable. Your phone calls or
e-mails are the best part of their day. And no
matter how tired or how busy your grandparents are, they're always up for the special
fun only a granddaughter can bring.

*What a grand thing
it is to be loved!
What a far grander
thing it is to love!*

Victor Hugo

Joanne had a hard time saying no to seeing her grandchildren, but the evening proved to be more of a challenge than she had anticipated.

acts of love

Joanne rushed around the kitchen trying to get a hurried pot of meat sauce on the stove before her husband got home. She didn't always try to have supper on time—they had grown accustomed to eating out after work. But tonight she had so much to do at home that she had left work early and told her husband, Jim, that she might as well put something on for the two of them. After teaching school for many years, she loved the fact that her new schedule could be more flexible. Still, the bookkeeping responsibilities for their family-owned hardware store now rested heavily on her shoulders, and it seemed no matter how much she accomplished at the office, there was always more to do after working hours.

I don't know if I should be thankful for computers or angry they were ever invented, she thought as she looked at the laptop resting on the kitchen table, waiting for her to begin the night's work.

"Don't look at me like that!" Joanne warned the beckoning computer. "I have to finish supper, bake a cake, work on my Sunday-school lesson, clean the house, and wash a load of clothes before you even get opened." She smiled at herself for talking to a machine as she dumped a can of tomato sauce over the browned ground sausage.

The sudden musical tones from her cell phone startled her out of her harried concentration. She wiped her hands and fumbled through the clutter in her purse to retrieve the phone.

"Hello," she answered, trying not to sound like the interruption was unwelcome.

"Mimi?" said a faint little voice on the other end of the line.

"Sissy, is that you?" Joanne asked, knowing it was her seven-year-old granddaughter.

"It's me!" Sissy said, louder and more confident now that she knew she had dialed the right number.

"Hi, sweetheart, what are you doing?" Joanne asked, trying to hold the phone with her chin and shoulder while grabbing a cake mix from the pantry.

"Can I spend the night? Can I?" Sissy asked in her sweetest tone—the one that rarely received a negative reply.

But this was a night Joanne had over committed herself already. Not wanting to turn her down directly, she decided to take another approach. "Sissy, Mimi has to bake a cake for Mrs. Potter, who is sick, and take it to her house."

"I don't care," came the quick reply.

"Sissy, Mimi has to get the house cleaned and the clothes washed, because tomorrow night after work, I'm having company for dinner," Joanne tried again, wondering briefly why she always talked to her granddaughter in third person.

The sweet little voice came back undaunted. "I don't care."

Joanne offered one last excuse. "You know it's a school night, and you'll have to get in bed pretty early."

"I don't care."

She had met her match. Joanne smiled and at last gave in as she thought of Sissy's toothless grin and deep dimples. "Well, it's a date then. Go get Mommy and let me see if she'll bring you over."

"Hang on, I'll go get her!" Sissy said. Joanne imagined Sissy's brown ponytail bouncing with each step as she ran to find her mom.

As she'd been talking to Sissy, Joanne had poured the mix in to the bowl and added the water and three eggs. Now she started the mixer, knowing she couldn't spare one minute waiting for her daughter to come to the phone. Her mind was racing, knowing that having Sissy would add to her already busy evening. She didn't really mind. Sissy wasn't any trouble. She just wanted to be able to spend some quality time with her, and tonight's schedule didn't leave much room for that.

"Mom, can you hear me?" Joanne's daughter was yelling into the phone over the whirring of the mixer.

"Oh, I'm sorry, Melanie. I was mixing a cake while Sissy was getting you. I've got to get this in the oven for Sandy. She's just home from the hospital."

"That's OK. Mom, I didn't know Sissy was calling you. Now that she's memorized your cell-phone number, you'll have to tell her no sometimes. You know she'd sleep over there every night if we'd let her."

Joanne smiled at her daughter's warning.

"It's OK, Melanie, she's never any trouble. I just don't like it when I can't relax and enjoy being with her. I've got a pretty full schedule tonight, but she's welcome to come whenever you can bring her." Joanne licked off a bit of cake mix that had landed on her knuckle.

"Actually, I was about to leave the house to pick up some milk, so I'll bring her right over. Are you sure you don't mind?"

"Of course I don't mind. See you soon."

Joanne had made so many cakes in her life, she could do it blindfolded. It only took a few minutes to spray the pan, pour in the batter, and shut the oven door. *Now to the laundry*, she thought as she washed her hands. But again the phone rang.

"Hey, Momma." Joanne's youngest daughter was on the line.

"Hi, babe, did you have a good day?" Joanne asked, knowing Rebecca's day involved two toddlers, and the answer could easily be no.

"Pretty good. The kids actually took naps at the same time. Can you believe it?"

"Now that is a good day! I used to love it when you and your sister napped at the same time. I thought I was on vacation!"

"Mom, I know this is short notice," Rebecca said sheepishly, "but I need some help with the kids tonight."

"What's going on?" Joanne asked.

"Remember my friend, Amy? She had her baby today, and I really need to go see her. Her mom can't come until the weekend. I won't be gone long."

"I'm really busy tonight, but if you can deliver a cake to Sandy's house for me on your way back home, I guess I can watch them for a little while." Joanne had a hard time saying no to seeing any of her grandchildren.

"Thanks, Mom. You're the best. I'll be there in about thirty minutes."

Joanne stirred the meat sauce one more time and went to collect the laundry. Hurrying back to the bathroom, she wondered where all that extra time was that she thought she'd have when the kids were grown. "Why can't Jim use a towel more than one time? My laundry duties would be cut in half if I could get that man to use a towel twice before throwing it on the floor. Oh well, you can't teach an old dog . . ." Joanne realized she was mumbling and shook her head as she gathered an armload of towels.

With the laundry started, Joanne returned to the kitchen. She opened the door of the refrigerator and then forgot why she had opened it.

Remembering it was the noodles she really wanted, she closed the refrigerator and headed for the pantry, thinking about an article she had read the night before about memory loss. *I should be cooking the foods mentioned in that article that would help my memory . . . if I could remember what they were,* she mused as she retrieved the pasta for her spaghetti supper.

"Mimi!" Sissy shrieked as she opened the back door. "I'm here!"

"Just in time to help me finish Papaw's supper.

Have you eaten?" Joanne reached down for a big hug from her granddaughter.

"Not yet," Sissy said as she gave her grandmother a giant squeeze.

"Hi, Mom." Melanie greeted Joanne with the usual peck on the cheek. "Here's her suitcase. I'll have the carpool pick her up at your house. Call me if you get too busy and need me to come get her, OK?"

"We'll be fine," Joanne reassured her daughter. "Sylvan and Sara will be over in a minute while Rebecca goes to the hospital to see a friend. Sissy can help watch them."

"Oh, Mom, are you sure?" Melanie placed both hands on her hips for emphasis.

"Like I said, we'll be fine!"

But the evening proved to be more challenging than Joanne had anticipated. It didn't take her long to realize that spaghetti wasn't the best dinner for toddlers, and she wondered if the kids actually got any noodles inside their mouths. After the meal the babies were into everything, and Joanne felt as though she spent the whole time cleaning up messes instead of enjoying her little ones. Sissy proved to be great help, but Joanne hated to keep asking her to entertain her cousins.

Two phone calls from friends at church and a

stopped-up sink didn't help matters, and by the time Rebecca came to pick up the two toddlers and the hastily frosted cake, Joanne was exhausted. She still had to help Sissy go over her spelling words and take a bath. She was thankful that at least her granddaughter's memory was still intact, and they were able to get through the words fairly quickly.

"Sissy, I'll run your bath water while you go get your suitcase," Joanne said, yawning and rubbing her aching back.

"JOANNE . . . telephone." Her husband called out over the sound of running water. "It's your mother."

Joanne knew this would be a long phone call, so she told Sissy to go ahead and bathe herself. Even though, at seven years old, Sissy was fully capable of doing that and washing her own hair, Joanne felt a twinge of guilt at not being able to help her. She reached over and pulled Sissy close to her. "I am so proud of you for being able to take care of yourself and for helping me with your cousins. After your bath, I'll read you a story," she promised.

The phone call took longer than Joanne expected, though, and soon she looked up to see a squeaky clean, wet-headed Sissy sitting beside her. She was already in her pajamas, so Joanne whispered that she needed to go ahead and get in bed and that she would be in soon. Sissy looked disappointed but shuffled off to the bedroom she always slept in.

When Joanne finished the conversation with her mother, she hurried off to check on Sissy. Her heart sank a little when she found Sissy already fast asleep, her angelic face surrounded by wet curls. She gathered up her wet hair so it wouldn't rest on her shoulders, straightened the blanket, and gave her a kiss.

"I'm sorry, sweetheart," she whispered in her granddaughter's ear. "We'll read a book next time."

Too tired to tackle the bookkeeping or the Sunday-school material, Joanne finished putting the dishes in the dishwasher and decided that now was a good time for her to soak in the tub. She turned the dimmer switch down in the bathroom and lit an aroma-therapy candle.

"Boy, do I need this," she said aloud, feeling the warm water graze her fingertips as she brought it to a good bath temperature.

Her large sunken bathtub was used more often as a mini-swimming pool by her grandchildren than as a comfort station for herself, but tonight it was her turn. She was feeling every bit of being a grandmother. Sylvan was a big two-year-old, and every time he came to visit, Joanne ended up feeling like she needed a trip to the chiropractor. She wiped up the sloshed water from Sissy's bath and gathered a clean towel and washcloth for herself.

She stepped into the tub and, with her eyes closed, settled down into the warmth that immediately relaxed her tired body. *Poor Sissy*, she thought. *All she wanted was a little attention.* She remembered her granddaughter's dejected expression. *I wish I could soak that away.* Joanne sighed and opened her eyes.

Through the steam, something red, blue, and yellow caught her attention. *Probably some leftover toys from the kids.* As she leaned forward, there on the side of the tub, just above the water level and written with colored-gel bath soaps, was a message: "I love you, Mimi."

Joanne could barely swallow the lump in her throat as she thought of the little girl lovingly and determinedly finding a way to connect with her grandmother. She smiled as a tear slipped down her cheek. No aroma therapy could match this. However hectic things got, nothing could interrupt the love between a grandmother and her granddaughter.

Understanding the Past

Chapter Two

Celebrate your differences. You are My treasured masterpiece. You can be confident that I'll always complete the unique work I've started in you.

Creatively,
Your Forever Faithful God

—from Romans 12:6; Ephesians 2:10; Philippians 1:6

Sometimes it's hard to understand the past—to see how it connects to the present and links inevitably to the future. But it does.

You, granddaughter, are the one who will carry on the traditions established by your grandparents and reinforced by your parents. You're an invaluable link in the family chain. You've heard stories and seen pictures that have the power to bring the stability of the past to the confusion of the present and the uncertainty of the future.

Your family is depending on you to hang on to those traditions. They're part of what identifies you as a family and gives you a distinctive bond. Perhaps you had an Indian grandmother who still

wore a sari on special occasions, or a grandfather who remembered the old Irish songs and sang
them with a thick brogue. Maybe your grandmother
always baked a coconut cake at Easter. Whatever the
traditions, you know the stories behind them. And you
strive to keep the family spirit alive—for yourself, your
children, and eventually your grandchildren.

Few things are more important to our future than
our past—especially how we use the lessons we've
learned to impact the world around us.

Granddaughter, as you preserve the parts
of your past, the memories flavored with
meaning, may they add as much rich-
ness to your life as you add to the
lives of those around you.

You are here
to enrich the world.
You impoverish
yourself if you forget
this errand.

Woodrow Wilson

"You look so beautiful," Jennifer's grandmother gushed. But Jennifer wrinkled her nose in disgust.

the art of being different

"Mom, it just doesn't matter," fourteen-year-old Jennifer Maddox yelled from the top of the staircase, straining to keep her voice within the limits she knew her mother would allow without dealing out punishment.

"It matters to me." Jennifer heard the exasperation in her mother's voice but chose to ignore it. She knew her mother was downstairs gathering up the last-minute items needed for the party, but Jennifer's mind was solely on her clothes.

"But you're the only one who cares! Nana never cares what I wear. Pleeeease!" Her plea seemed to fall on deaf ears. Her mother didn't even acknowledge her words.

Stomping back into her room, Jennifer grabbed the dress her mother had picked out for her and kicked off the army boots she had wanted to wear. "Why did I have to be born into this family," she grumbled to herself. "What a boring mother—she's never any fun!"

Her scowl faded a little as she caught a glimpse of herself in the mirror and paused to admire her reflection. Her new hairstyle with its short, bleached-and-spiked tips was perfect for her small face. She couldn't believe her uptight mother had agreed to let her get such a cool cut. Then she touched her newly pierced left ear. *I can't wait to show Nana*, she thought as she relished her success last Saturday: talking her mom into letting her have not just one but two holes in her left ear. *Now I'm getting somewhere*, she had thought. Today she was a little more cynical. *Mom must have been in a really good mood that day—unlike today, when she insists on my wearing this stupid dress!*

Somewhere in the back of Jennifer's mind, she knew she loved her mother very much. But they were so different. Jennifer's casual, slightly edgy attitude clashed with her mother's more reserved world-view. To say they approached life from different angles was an understatement, and tonight's showdown had been just one more in an endless series over the years.

"Jen, please hurry. Your grandma's party starts at seven, and I'm in charge of greeting the guests."

Jennifer took in a deep breath and rolled her eyes. *She's always in charge of something.* She reached over her head to finish zipping up her dress. *I wish she could just chill out for one day.*

"Time to go," her mom shouted from the end of the staircase. "I'll be in the car."

Jennifer took one more look in the mirror and muttered to herself. "What's so wrong with wanting to wear jeans instead of a dress? She thinks everyone should be just like she is. Doesn't she understand that I'm a person too?"

She spiked her hair a little higher, then stomped out of her bedroom. She made sure the door slammed behind her, knowing there was no one in the house to hear the sound of protest, but still feeling better for having done it.

The drive to her grandma's seventieth birthday party was silent except for the overflow of blaring music she defiantly made sure could be heard from her headset. She didn't want to risk a conversation with her mother. She bobbed her head up and down and back and forth to the beat and, for a moment, lost herself in the music.

"Jennifer, could you please turn the volume down. I can't hear myself think, and I'm not even wearing the earphones! You're going to lose your hearing one day." Jennifer rolled her eyes again and turned the volume down one level.

They arrived at the restaurant before any of the guests, but Jennifer's grandma, Judy, was already sitting in the reception area waiting for them. Jennifer loved her grandmother immensely. They shared a unique bond because they were both artists. Her grandma loved to paint and had introduced Jennifer to the world of color and design at an early age. To her grandmother's delight, Jennifer had taken to art naturally and showed promising talent. Together they had created many masterpieces—most decorating the retired woman's refrigerator but masterpieces just the same.

Jennifer greeted her grandmother with a big hug. "Nana, what do you think of my haircut?"

Judy held Jennifer by the shoulders at arm's length to get a good look. "Why, I think it looks just like you," she answered diplomatically. "You always look beautiful to me. And what's that I see in your ear?"

"Isn't it cool? Mom let me do it last weekend. Everyone's getting their ears pierced multiple times."

Now Jennifer's mother rolled her eyes. "You always say to pick your battles," she said with a resigned smile. "Happy birthday, Mom." She gave her mother a hug.

"Thank you, sweetheart. It's wonderful of you and your brother to do this for me. I hope you didn't go to too much trouble."

"Nonsense! You couldn't turn seventy without a

party. We've been looking forward to this evening. If you'll excuse me for just a minute, I need to check with the manager to make sure everything's ready. Call me picky, but I just can't leave anything to chance. I'll be right back."

"Jennifer, you look so beautiful," Jennifer's grandmother gushed as she motioned for her granddaughter to sit beside her.

Jennifer wrinkled her nose in disgust. "Mom made me wear this dress. I had picked out the coolest black shirt and jeans to wear. And I have a new belt that hangs really low on my hips. But you know Mom, she said I had to look 'nice.' I thought it *did* look nice."

"Yes, I know your mom. I raised her." She chuckled. "And on some days, that was quite a challenge."

"It was?" Jennifer's eyes widened as she waited for the inside scoop on her "perfect" mother.

"You bet. We're just so different. No matter how hard I pushed, she hated art classes. And to be honest, she was never very good—couldn't draw a stick figure. You know, Jennifer, God has given you a gift in your artistic ability. I've seen it from the time you were two years old."

Jennifer could already feel her spirits rise. Her grandmother always had a way of making her feel good about herself.

"Did you and Mom fight about everything?" she

pleaded, wanting more details.

"Well, not everything. You know, it's important to remember that God has made each of us uniquely special. Your mother has many talents I don't have—like organizing and taking charge of things. Sure, I would have liked it if she had been artistic, but what I really wanted was for her to be herself. It's the same with you and your mom—you both have wonderful qualities, they're just different. And that means the things you like to do or the clothes you choose to wear can come into conflict."

"Tell me about it," Jennifer mumbled and hung her head.

Her grandmother lifted Jennifer's face and looked her in the eye. "But Jennifer, don't ever doubt that your mother wants the same for you that I wanted for her—to be your best self. There will be times when you don't agree on things, but those little differences are just about style and individual taste. They have nothing to do with your mother's love for you and her pride in you. Those are unchanging."

Jennifer's shoulders remained slumped. "I know you're probably right, but why doesn't she like anything I like, when you like everything I like?"

Her grandmother smiled sagely. "You have to remember, your mom is the one in the responsible position, while I get to just join in for the fun! When I was raising your mom, I was the one who had to be responsible. That's a much tougher job.

"Speaking of fun . . ." Jennifer's grandmother reached down and pulled a little package from her purse. "I brought you something."

"Nana, I'm the one who's supposed to bring *you* a gift. It's your birthday!" Jennifer laughed with glee at the surprise.

"It's my birthday, and I can give a gift if I want to. After all, it is more fun to give than to receive." She handed Jennifer a tiny box wrapped in pink paper and tied with a black bow.

"I love pink and black! You're the coolest grandmother ever." Jennifer opened the package and was thrilled to find a new set of pierced earrings—and one extra earring.

"Oh, Nana, they're perfect. I can't wait until I can take out these studs and wear these new earrings. But how did you know I had gotten my ears pierced? I just told you tonight."

Her grandmother smiled and replied with a wink. "Your mother called me and told me how excited you were and how cute you looked. She's really not such a bad mom after all, now is she?"

Jennifer looked down at the earrings and then at

her grandmother. "I guess you're right." Her lips curled up in a smile. "But I'm still glad you're around to be fun with!"

"Me too," her grandmother said. "Now let's go to a party!"

Staying
Connected

Chapter Three

Call upon Me and I'll answer you. Find comfort in My ancient ways. My unfailing love is your solace. No matter what, I'm committed to you! I'm always watching over your life.

Loving you always,
Your God of All Comfort

—from Jeremiah 33:3; Psalm 119:52, 76; Deuteronomy 31:6; Psalm 121:8; 2 Corinthians 1:3

In the hustle and bustle of your day, amid all the exciting challenges in your life, you probably sometimes feel you don't have the time to keep up with family—to make that phone call or write that letter. But you do it anyway, because as a granddaughter you know the importance of staying connected to the people who love you and whom you love.

It's said that no man is an island, and you know that's true. As you navigate through life with its twists and turns, you and your grandparents have been there for each other. Whether it's their cheers at a ball game or their birthday cards with an extra ten dollars in them, your holiday visits or your phone calls just to say hi, you share a special bond with them because you are a special grand-daughter.

Staying connected is easier today than when your grandparents were children, but it still takes time, effort, and care. Maybe even more so because we're all moving so fast it's hard to slow down and take time for relationships. But when we do, we weave a rich tapes-try of love. That's a lesson you learned from your grandparents, and it's a blessing you give back to them every time you call, write, or e-mail just to say I love you.

Sure, times have changed. But with wonderful granddaughters like you, staying connected remains a time-less treasure.

If I can put one touch of rosy sunset into the life of any man or woman, I shall feel that I have worked with God.

♦

George MacDonald

Missy put her head in her hands, feeling close to tears. "Working in New York is something I've always wanted to do. Why am I feeling so torn all of a sudden?"

the comfort quilt

Missy meandered through her grandmother's house, acutely aware of her surroundings. Rubbing her fingers along the antique dining-room table, she thought of the many meals she had eaten there. Even now her grandmother was in the kitchen preparing a special dinner for her. The humming she heard over the chopping and dicing was her grandma's favorite hymn. The scent, overpowering even the cinnamon potpourri synonymous with her grandmother's inviting home, was from Missy's favorite dish, roast beef. She stopped for a moment to savor the aroma, her mouth watering in anticipation.

And He walks with me and He talks with me. Silently, Missy filled in the words to the tune coming from the kitchen. *Mamaw has taught me so much*, she thought as she continued her farewell tour through the house. She looked over the dining-room table, past the antique furniture and accents perfectly arranged to break up the long space across the front of the house, to the far side of the living room. *I'll bet I could make it to the couch blindfolded.*

For twenty-four years she had been a part of this house. She had played dominoes and checkers on every tabletop, hide-and-seek in every closet and under every bed. She'd dressed up dolls and pushed them in their miniature strollers from one room to the next. Missy closed her eyes. This was as good a time as any to try her walk of faith. She set off toward the couch. Within seconds she had reached the sofa unhindered and sat down, snuggling a pillow to her chest and breathing in the clean, familiar smell.

Hours on this couch, she thought. Scenes of late-night talks with her grandmother ran through her mind: When she was six, she had asked her grandmother what happens when pets die. As a teenager she had cried to her about awful dates. She'd done countless homework assignments stretched out here. More recently she had announced with excitement—and a little fear—the job offer in New York City. How encouraging and assuring her grandmother had been.

Why am I feeling so torn all of a sudden? Working in New York is something I've always wanted to do. I can't back out now. Missy put her head in her hands, feeling close to tears.

"Missy," her grandmother called out. "Would you set the table for me? I'm running a little behind."

Missy took a deep breath and straightened her back, forcing herself back into composure. "Sure, give me a minute. I'm just checking on a few things."

She stood up and started back toward the dining room but couldn't help pausing when she caught sight of the quilt rack. Her grandmother always had a handmade quilt hanging there, waiting to be given to someone who needed special care. Her family had dubbed them comfort quilts. Growing up, Missy had watched her grandmother quilt her way through every triumph and tragedy. She quilted for the birth of new babies, and she quilted for friends who were hospital bound. Missy couldn't help but walk over and finger the edges. The needlework seemed to represent everything her grandmother stood for: courage, hospitality, resourcefulness, caring. For some reason, tonight the quilt felt almost magical. Missy had never really paid much attention to the pattern or the choice of fabrics. But tonight she noticed. The varying shades of blue had been stitched together masterfully, each shade complementing the others.

Wow, this one is really beautiful. I love blue. I can't believe I never had Mamaw teach me to quilt. She sighed deeply, feeling suddenly remorseful at the lost opportunity, then joined her grandmother in the kitchen.

Staying Connected

"What was that?" her grandmother asked.

"Oh, nothing, Mamaw. Everything smells wonderful!" She gave her grandmother a kiss on the cheek. "Thank you for doing this for me. I'm going to miss this so much!"

"It's a labor of love." Her grandmother returned the kiss. "And don't go acting like you won't be back. Any time you're in town, this kitchen will be open for service. Right now we had better hurry. Your parents will be here in fifteen minutes, and we're not quite ready. You know how your daddy hates to wait!"

Missy smiled as she thought of her dad coming in, removing the lid from the roast, and saying, "Smells good, when do we eat?"

"Let's use the good china tonight," her grandmother suggested. "You know where everything is."

Missy went to the dining room and carefully lifted the plates from the china cabinet. Once her grandma had explained how Grampa had surprised her with the china on their fifteenth wedding anniversary. He had shopped and shopped, looking for the perfect pattern to surprise his wife. As Missy peered at her reflection in the cream-colored plates with their gold rims, she thought her grandpa had done a great job. *It must not look a day older than it did when Grandma opened the original box.* She raised an eyebrow. *Of course, it's not like it should be worn out from overuse. I'll bet I could count on my fingers how many times I've seen these plates out. Special occasions, that's it.* Suddenly it sunk in that this time *she* was the special occasion.

"Oh, Missy," her grandma called from the kitchen. "Can you also set out the silverware? A few spoons are missing, but there should be enough."

Missy grinned. She knew the missing spoons were probably her doing back when she was a child holding pretend tea parties.

Just then she heard the front door open and a loud "Mmm-mm. Something sure smells good! When do we eat?"

Missy shook her head and laughed. *There's Dad.*

"How about a hug and then I'll think about putting food on the table?" she heard her grandma say. "First things first!"

"That's what I was talking about. First things first. Where's the food?"

Missy hung back, listening to the familiar banter. *That, I will miss. It's hard to capture that in a letter or an e-mail.*

"Hey, Mom and Dad." Missy went to the kitchen and hugged each of her parents.

"What do I need to do?" her mom asked as she washed her hands, preparing to help.

Missy's grandmother directed her answer at her son, who was picking at the roast with a fork. "We're just waiting on the rolls."

"All right, all right. Can I help it if I think you're a fabulous cook? Do you want me to carve the roast?"

"Yes, if you think you can keep from eating the whole thing in the process!"

Soon the roast was on the table, the rolls were buttered, and the family was seated and talking animatedly about the adventures of their week. Missy soaked in every detail, relishing the laughter and love that filled the room. Finally, she cleared her throat. "Can I have your attention please?" She swallowed hard, not wanting to cry just yet.

"I know I'm not leaving for a few days, but I've been thinking about what it means to be part of a family that loves and supports you. And I've concluded it means everything. Tonight I got here early because I wanted some quiet time alone in this house, touching, smelling, and remembering everything I've done here.

"There's something extraordinary about a grandparent's house that I can't quite explain. It's like your own house because you feel like everything is yours, yet you're treated like a special guest. I want to thank you, Mamaw, for the heritage of a family whose greatest tradition is to love one another. It all started with you and Grandpa. You two passed it on to Daddy, and he and Mom have taught me. I just want you all to know that no matter where I am, you are the most important people in the world to me, and I love you."

Missy's mother picked up a napkin and dabbed away a tear. Her dad pretended to be clearing his throat. Missy's grandmother was the first to speak, her voice thick with emotion. "Well, if I can manage it, I have something special to share too." The room got even quieter as she got up and walked over to stand behind Missy.

Missy closed her eyes, sure she couldn't hold back tears much longer.

"You all know how much I love this little girl." Her grandmother patted Missy on the shoulder as if she were still five years old. "I know she's all grown up, but she's still my little Missy. Her decision to move to New York is a brave one, and I want her to know how proud I am of her adventurous spirit and her desire to make her own way. But she's right—family is the most precious gift we have. So I have something for you—for the days when you're missing that family connection and you need someone to wrap loving arms around you and hold you tight." She made her way over to the quilt rack.

Missy held her breath as her grandmother picked up the quilt and began unfolding it with as much care and ceremony as a marine unfolding the American flag. As she exposed each layer, the hours of work it had obviously taken, the tiny stitches that formed an intricate design, were evidence of how she loved Missy.

Missy rose and wrapped her arms around her grandmother, quilt and all. "Oh, Mamaw, this is for me? It's the best gift ever!"

"Wait," her grandmother said with a gleam in her eye. "You haven't seen the best part."

Missy helped her grandmother unfold the quilt the rest of the way. When it was open, her grandmother instructed her to turn it over and look at the other side.

Missy gasped. She couldn't believe her eyes. Right in the middle of the quilt was a collage of pictures that had been scanned onto the individual squares of fabric—Missy and her parents and grandparents at various stages of their lives. Now the tears were unstoppable, and Missy grabbed her grandmother again in a tight embrace. Their special bond had been captured forever in the most beautiful quilt she had ever seen. Now, no matter where she was, all she had to do to feel at home was touch the comfort quilt.

Feeling
Loved

Chapter Four

You can't begin to measure My love for you.
It's even better than life. I keep My covenant
of love to a thousand generations. You can count
on My goodness and love every day.

Eternal hugs,
Your God of Love

—from Psalms 103:11; 63:3; Deuteronomy 7:9; Psalm 23:6

Isn't it fun to be the center of attention? Whether it's your kindergarten graduation or your wedding day, you are *it*! All the cameras and lights are on you.

But special occasions only come along once in a while. Want to enjoy that special place of importance every day? You don't have to climb Mount Everest or win a beauty contest. You don't have to prove or earn anything. You are a granddaughter.

The moment you came into this world, you changed your grandparents' lives forever— just by being you. You give them someone to love, someone to shower attention on and to delight in. And the best thing is it doesn't have to be a special day, like a graduation or a wedding, for you to be the most important person in the world to them. It can just be any day and anytime—it's every day and all the time.

You are reason enough for celebration—no special occasion needed. It doesn't matter what you look like or how talented you are or what anyone else thinks of you. Your grandparents think you're perfect just the way you are. Their hearts were given to you on an unconditional silver platter the minute you were born. No matter what else happens, you, granddaughter, hold an irrevocable place of importance in their hearts.

The measure of
God's love
is that He loves
without measure.

St. Bernard

Everything was in place
for the wedding
of her dreams.
There had been no
snags . . . until now.

in sickness
and in health

Shelly looked at her fresh set of French-manicure sculpted nails. *If they weren't so lovely, I'd bite them right off.* She was so nervous that her old nail-biting habit had returned with a vengeance. But her grandmother had treated her and her bridesmaids to manicures the day before, and now as she placed her hands delicately on the white skirt of her wedding gown, her thoughts again returned to her grandma.

This can't be happening. She sighed and started pacing the floor of the tiny bride's room.

There had been no snags until now. The flowers were the exact color she wanted. The bridesmaids' dresses fit perfectly. The rehearsal had gone smoothly. Everything was in place for the wedding of her dreams, and she knew the credit went to her grandmother, who had poured countless hours of love and energy into making this day as wonderful as even a princess could have wished.

Shelly's grandmother had been a much sought-after wedding planner. Mothers had loved her attention to detail, and fathers her ability to work magic with any wedding budget. When she retired ten years earlier, she had promised Shelly she would come out of retirement to plan her only granddaughter's wedding. Since Shelly was a girl, they had poured over bride magazines together, picking out the perfect flowers and designing and redesigning wedding cakes—all in anticipation of the day Shelly would walk down the aisle in a fairy-tale setting created by her grandmother.

But just a few hours ago, Shelly's mother had tapped her gently on the shoulder. "Shelly, I don't want you to panic. Everything is OK. I just have to tell you something."

Speechless, Shelly had just stared at her mother. Surely those words on your wedding day would seem the perfect time to panic. The possibilities were swirling in her imagination: the cake falling on its way to the church, the church catching fire from a stray candle, the photographer not showing up . . .

"Don't panic!" She remembered her voice catching somewhere in her throat before squeaking out. "What does that mean? What happened?" She had tried to stay calm, but a sickening feeling had taken hold of her stomach almost instantly.

"Your grandpa just called, and Grandma is at the hospital. She wasn't feeling well when she woke up this morning, but she just kept going to make sure everything was ready for tonight."

Shelly's eyes widened as she listened to the details, now focused on her grandmother's health and not yet considering the impact the news would have on her own plans. Her mother continued. "She was talking to the florist one last time when nausea overcame her, and she became very sick."

"She'll be OK by the wedding, won't she?" The expression in her voice was seeking confirmation rather than an answer to a question.

"Well, honey," Shelly's mom responded guardedly, "Grandpa said he took her on to the hospital hoping they could give her something to get her through the wedding, but he said he wasn't sure it would work."

Somewhere in the middle of her concern for her grandmother's health, it hit her. The candles were only minutes away from being lit, the finishing touches of pink roses were being added to the three-tier cake— and her wedding planner was in the hospital.

"Oh, Mom." Shelly bit her lip. "She's the one who knows everything. When the music starts, who wears a corsage, when the candle lighters start—"

Feeling Loved

"We'll be just fine," Shelly's mom said reassuringly. "We practiced last night, and everyone knows what to do. Besides, I've heard your grandmother say many times, 'You can't mess up a wedding.'"

Shelly could hear her grandmother's voice in those words, and she relaxed a little, but she still didn't like the thought of her strong, always proper grandma on a gurney in the emergency room. The matriarch of their family stood five feet, ten inches tall, with piercing blue eyes and Clairol-brown hair. No one ever suspected she was seventy-five years old. She was a tower of strength to Shelly—someone she called whenever she needed sound, no-nonsense advice.

"Mom, remember last night when Grandma insisted on bringing a fruit tray to have here for the bridesmaids to munch on? I'll bet she's thinking about that right now. She wanted everything to be so perfect."

"I'm sure you're right." Her mom shook her head and smiled. "She's probably still trying to figure out how she can get a fruit tray up here. Grandpa said to tell you she whispered between waves of nausea, 'Tell Shelly not to worry. At six o' clock, I'll be there!'"

Shelly's lip quivered as she thought of her sweet grandmother, with whom she had shared so many of her wedding dreams, not being able to see it all come true. She closed her eyes and said a prayer for her grandmother's health.

"Mom, should we postpone the wedding for an hour or so? Grandma would be so sad if she missed it. What should we do?"

"Sweetie, it's too late to change the schedule now. The music will start at six o'clock, and you will walk down the aisle just as you and your grandmother planned." Shelly's mom reached over and grabbed her worried daughter's hand. "She had everything organized; the wedding will go smoothly and be lovely. Your grandmother will be sad if she misses it, but she would be beside herself if she knew you were even thinking of delaying it because of her. Grandpa said she'll be fine and for us to not worry. Now let's get downstairs for pictures."

Shelly hoped and prayed that her smile didn't look too fixed in the photo session as she tried to remain calm and not focus too much on her grandma's illness. She had made her mother promise to keep her updated if any news came in.

The last call her mother received was at four o'clock, and Shelly's grandmother was being released but was still very sick. "Dad, tell her to go straight home and rest. The wedding will be videotaped, and she can watch it later."

Shelly was listening to her mother talk and

Feeling Loved

wanted to agree with her, yet she couldn't help wishing her grandmother would come to the wedding. After all the years of planning, it was almost unthinkable to go through it without her.

Shelly looked at her watch. Five-fifteen. *She's not going to make it. How can I get married without Grandma?*

Just then the door opened and her mother appeared. "They want us to start lining up. Are you ready?"

Shelly knew her mom was doing her best to be cheerful and positive and to ensure that her special day wasn't ruined.

"Sure, Mom," Shelly said, blinking back a tear.

"Let me have one last hug before I have to share you forever with the man of your dreams." Her mom held her extra tight as she whispered, "Here's a hug from your grandmother. She'll love the pictures. You look beautiful!"

"Thank you, Momma." Shelly sniffled and took a deep breath. "I'm ready. I guess that old saying is true: 'The best laid plans of mice and men often go awry.' I sure didn't expect Grandma to miss this wedding, but I know it'll be OK."

"That's my girl! You know, your grandmother would say wild horses couldn't keep her from being at your wedding. You know she'd be here if she could."

Shelly's mom walked behind her to hold the long, beaded train in the air as Shelly walked down the hall and into the foyer of the church building. Shelly clung to her flowers and nervously played with her engagement ring as she practiced the timing of her steps, mentally humming the wedding march.

Her dad greeted her at the back of the chapel. "Where did my little girl go?" he asked as he kissed her cheek. "I haven't seen such a beautiful bride since your mother took my breath away twenty-five years ago." Seeing her stoic father tear up surprised her and tore at her heart.

"Oh, Daddy—" She returned her dad's kiss and smiled as she wiped the faint lipstick smudge off his cheek. "I love you so much."

The bridesmaids were taking their slow walk toward the stained-glass front of the chapel. Shelly could see that the little sanctuary was almost full with her family and friends. Everything was perfect. *Grandma would have loved this.*

Suddenly the music changed, and she felt her father's nudge to move up to the archway where their walk would begin. She caught her breath as she saw everyone stand and face her. This was it—the moment she had dreamed of.

Shelly smiled as her dad patted her arm. She felt almost as if she were gliding down the aisle on a magic

Feeling Loved

carpet, her gaze meeting that of her husband-to-be. Then, as if by impulse, she looked toward the pew where her grandparents were to be seated—and discovered, to her surprise, that they were right where they were supposed to be, smiling and crying!

She couldn't make herself keep walking. She had to stop and hug her grandma. "Grandma, what are you doing? I thought you were going home after they released you!"

"I promised you I'd be here at six o'clock. Wild horses couldn't have kept me from sharing this day with you!"

Shelly laughed and took her place again beside her dad. As she started back down the aisle, she mouthed "I love you" to her grandmother. She didn't have to wait for her grandmother to mouth it back. She already knew.

Being Supportive

Chapter Five

Even before you ask, I know your needs. I am able to provide all of your needs according to My unlimited riches in glory. You can wait in hope for Me because I'm your help and your protection.

Supporting you,
Your Heavenly Father

—from Matthew 6:8; Philippians 4:19; Psalm 33:20

Only a handful of people know almost everything about you. It's a small minority that knows whether you eat spinach or like scary movies. Your parents, maybe your best friend . . . and your grandparents. Having people around who know you so well that they can sense a need and act on it is one of the best feelings in the world, and that's just the kind of feeling a grandparent-granddaughter relationship can bring.

Yet you've never allowed yourself to stay only on the receiving end of your grandparents' affection. You give your amazing love and support to them as well. And through the years, they've come to know they can depend on you. Your love for them and your concern for their well-being is evident and invaluable. While they would do anything for you, what's even more special is knowing you would do anything for them.

That's what a support system is. It sustains you through good times and bad. Whether it's late at night or early in the morning, you're there for each other.

Today's society is mobile, and grandparents may be more active for longer than ever before—traveling, taking classes, or launching second careers. But they still need you and want to be part of your life. A loving, supportive relationship with you, their granddaughter, is a joy and a blessing.

*The smallest seed
of faith is better than
the largest fruit
of happiness.*

♦

Henry David Thoreau

Anne chased her giggling, diaper-trailing toddler down the hall. "What am I doing wrong?" she lamented.

the dinner guest

Anne was up to her ears in poop. Well, almost. She had a baby in diapers, a toddler being potty trained, and two cats that had suddenly developed an aversion to their litter pan. Sometimes she felt as though her entire day revolved around cleaning something up.

Today had been no different, and she was exhausted. But finally, for a few precious minutes, the house was relatively quiet. Two-year-old Jesse was entertaining himself in his room; baby Gracie was sitting quietly on Anne's lap, and the cats had been put out to wander in the yard. Anne wouldn't have been too disappointed if they wandered away entirely.

She had just picked up a novel she was determined to read when the phone rang. Anne sighed. She was tired of all the telemarketing calls and was sorely tempted to ignore it—to launch her own personal phone strike. But she put the book down, hiked Gracie on one hip, and picked up the receiver. *Maybe it's Calgon calling to take me away*, she thought wryly.

"Hi, Anne, this is Granny. How are you?"

"Oh, Granny. Hi! I'm fine. How are you?" It was almost as good as Calgon. Anne loved the sound of her grandmother's voice. It was so soothing and always sincere.

"Well, honey, I'm doing pretty well. I just wanted to see how my babies were."

"They're great too. But Granny, I think I started this whole process too late. You had your babies young, when you had lots of energy. I thought after running an office, motherhood would be easy. I had no idea how hard this could be."

Granny Grace laughed. "I seem to recall someone who said having babies in her thirties would mean she'd be more mature and able to handle it." Even when she was teasing, Anne could hear the sympathy in her grandmother's voice.

"Did I say that? What was I thinking?" Anne laughed too, knowing it was the truth. "Although I seem to recall someone saying, 'You're probably right!'"

Granny Grace sighed in happy resignation. "You know I'll support you, whatever you say."

"I know. Really, the kids are great. Jesse's ear infection cleared up, and Gracie is growing like a little weed."

Just then Jesse came running through the house with his diaper in hand and its contents spilling on the floor.

"What am I doing wrong?" she lamented into the phone. "Here comes Jesse with his diaper off, leaving a trail for me to clean up. I guess I'd better go. I love you. We'll talk soon. Maybe we can go to lunch later this week."

Anne barely heard her grandmother's reply as she hung up the phone and went after Jesse. "Stop, right this minute," she yelled as she chased a giggling Jesse down the hall. *Why didn't I ask Granny how she potty trained nine kids and lived to tell about it?*

Catching her energetic toddler with one hand while clinging to the baby with the other hand wasn't an easy task. Now she had to figure out how to get everyone clean and supper on the table by six o'clock. Her husband, Jack, had been out of town on business, and she'd promised him a home-cooked meal on his return. She wanted to tell him it would be much easier if he brought home pizza, but he never quite understood how busy her days were. Those few lines she got to read in her novel constituted the only break she'd had the entire day.

Looking at her watch, she realized it was already four thirty and time was running out. *What do I have in the freezer*, she thought as she scrubbed the wood floor for the third time that day. *Maybe the ham is still in there from Christmas. I could thaw it in the microwave . . .*

The phone rang again. Anne got up from her knees and made her way into the kitchen once again. *I'm too old for this.*

"Hello," she answered, trying to sound more pleasant than she felt.

"Hi, honey! How's your day going? It's really been busy at the office. I got back in around noon, and you know how hard it is to play catch-up."

Anne stood with a Lysol can in one hand and a mop in the other as she listened to her husband's cheerful voice. "Same here," she managed to say. "Just as busy as little bees!"

"Great," Jack chirped. "I can't wait to see you guys. I hope you don't mind, but since you were cooking tonight anyway, I asked Donnie from accounting to come for dinner. We've been trying to get together on that project for a week now, and I figured tonight's as good a night as any."

Anne's silence spoke volumes, but Jack didn't notice. "Are you still there? Can you hear me?"

"I'm here. What time did you want to eat?" Anne's voice was as frosty as an old freezer.

"I was thinking we would come a little early so we don't have to work too late," Jack replied, seemingly oblivious to his wife's dilemma. "How about five-thirty? He's single, so don't worry too much about the house. He'll just be happy for a home-cooked meal."

"Great, see you soon." Anne put the phone rather firmly in its cradle and added sarcastically, "Oh, you mean he won't mind a little mess on the floor as long as I have some good food?"

She finished cleaning the hallway and went to the laundry room to put away her cleaning supplies. *I will remain calm . . . I will remain calm . . .* she began chanting in her head.

The sound of splashing water caught her attention, and she bolted into the bathroom to find Gracie tottering over the toilet, the water just within her reach, having the time of her life.

"Oh, Gracie, no, no. The potty isn't a toy." But Gracie didn't agree and managed one more splash before Anne whisked her away.

Anne sat Gracie on the bathroom counter and lathered her down with soap. Gracie dangled her little feet in the sink, finding another new game to play.

As she watched her daughter in the mirror, Anne couldn't resist smiling at the chubby little face and beautiful brown eyes looking back at her. Her hair was soaked and formed one little curl on her forehead.

"OK, you are adorable, but your daddy is expecting dinner in forty-five minutes, and I haven't even started!"

"Come on, you little monkey. Let's get some clean clothes on you, and then I have to think about supper."

Anne smoothed baby lotion on Gracie, put pajamas on her, and placed her in the highchair with a handful of Cheerios on the tray. "There, now you'll stay out of trouble for a while. I'm not so sure about your brother."

She headed back down the hall to check on Jesse, but before she reached his bedroom, the doorbell rang. Anne sighed, rolling her eyes in despair. "What now?" She peeked in Jesse's room, not wanting him to see her, and was thrilled to see that he was still quietly playing. She tip-toed backward and then headed for the front door. "If this is a vacuum-cleaner salesman, I will not be responsible for my actions," she warned no one in particular.

"Granny, what are you doing here?" Anne exclaimed, surprised at this unexpected visit. "Come in!"

"We didn't get to finish our conversation earlier, so I decided to come on over anyway." Anne's mouth dropped opened as she watched her grandmother waltz past with her hands full of potholders and saucepans. "I fixed your family some dinner. I called to tell you, but those babies were keeping you too busy to listen. Anyway, when your grandpa was alive, he used to say, 'Don't ask if you can help, just go ahead and do it.' So here I am. I hope you don't mind. If you've already made something, you can just save this for tomorrow. There's nothing here that won't keep."

Anne was speechless. *How could she know?* Her eyes welled up with tears of relief and gratitude as she hugged her grandmother. "Granny, you will never know how much I needed this tonight," she whispered.

"Oh, I think I already do. I'm not too old to remember—been there, done that!"

They shared a good laugh and, arm in arm, headed to the car to unload the rest of the dinner.

Facing the Unknown

Chapter Six

When you face the unknown, seek Me and I'll answer you, delivering you from all your fears. When you look to Me, you'll shine. Come to me with all of your worries, because I care deeply for you. Find the secret of being joyful in hope, patient in trouble, and faithful in prayer.

Guiding you,
Your God of Hope

—from Psalm 34:4–5; 1 Peter 5:7; Romans 12:12

Contemplating the future can be fun, but sometimes it can also be frightening. Years ago explorers made their way over treacherous mountains or through dangerous woodlands to secure their future family homes. They were willing to risk their very lives to guarantee a better future for their children and grandchildren.

Times have changed, and we rarely have to risk our lives to make sure of our future. Still, the uncertainty of where our future might take us can be scary. Generations have gone before you, but you'll need to make your own mark on the world. You probably won't be called on to forge your way through the wilderness, but you still must

navigate the rough terrain of choices that will
determine the course of your life.

Daunting, isn't it? You may wonder if you're ready
to forge ahead into the unknown.

You are.

You've watched those who have gone before you.
Their experience has been your training. It's never
easy to accept responsibility, to realize that others
are now looking to you as the pioneer who will
clear a path for them. But Granddaughter,
face the future with confidence, knowing
that you are loved. That you will
always be in our hearts. That
whatever life demands, you
can do it.

Every experience
God gives us,
every person He puts
in our lives, is the
perfect preparation
for the future
that only He can see.

◆

Corrie ten Boom

The left turn into the
driveway nearly took
her breath away
as she realized how
unprepared she was
for this moment.

love remembers

The short one-hour trip from Alexandria to Natchitoches, Louisiana, felt instead like a tedious cross-country journey. Kaitlyn's eyelids were leaden from lack of sleep, but her heart was even heavier. She blinked hard to try to bring some moisture back into her tired eyes and struggled to think of something besides Grandma and Grandpa Jones.

It was no use. She couldn't help reliving the many trips she had taken to that house. She thought of the big family van, coloring books, markers, sticker activities, and tiny cars strewn about on the floor. Her mom had tried everything to keep sibling squabbles to a minimum. Eagerly anticipating a week or weekend of Grandma's good cooking and Grandpa's fishing trips, Kaitlyn and her brothers could hardly contain their energy and excitement.

Even now she could almost smell bacon frying and Grandma's homemade biscuits fresh and hot. "You can just pick them up with your fingers and sop them in the syrup," her grandma would tell them. Kaitlyn's mouth watered involuntarily at the most delicious memory of all, the wonderful scent of fresh pecan pie wafting from the oven. She sighed, weighed down with the knowledge that she would never experience days like that again.

She looked right and left to cross an intersection and became conscious of how much the landscape had changed in the thirty years she'd been traveling this small, two-lane highway. The trees were bigger, the gas stations more frequent, and the traffic heavier. *Everything changes.*

Her parents had gone to the house the day before, but Kaitlyn couldn't get off work until the weekend. Her brothers would come when they could get free from jobs and other obligations. But as the oldest grandchild and the only girl, Kaitlyn always felt more responsible to help out.

She turned on the radio to the local Christian station, looking for some comfort. A remix of "I Come to the Garden Alone" was playing, and soon Kaitlyn's eyes were full of tears as she thought of her grandmother's sweet voice singing with the other fifty or so church members on Sundays. No megachurch for her grandmother. "I don't need a lot of folks around me to know I'm doing the right thing," her grandma had told her once. "I just need me and the Lord to worship." Kaitlyn smiled. Her grandmother's dedicated faith had influenced their whole family.

A pothole jarred her to attention, and she realized she was almost to the water tower. "I see it." "I saw it first!" "You didn't call it!" She could hear echoes of the van full of kids arguing about who saw the tower first. They all knew it meant they were just minutes away from Grandma's house.

Natchitoches was the oldest city in the Louisiana Purchase. One downtown street was still made of the original bricks. The Cane River meandered right down the center of the sleepy little town. Kaitlyn's brothers would line up on the riverbank, fishing with Grandpa, while she and her grandmother wiled away the hours browsing in antique stores and eating ice cream. Most of their evenings were spent the same way each trip, frying the fish the boys had caught and laughing about how many hooks Grandpa had to get out of a tree or a floating limb.

Kaitlyn turned right automatically and admired the row of pecan trees that always welcomed her to Grandma's house. *No wonder she baked so many pecan pies.* She breathed in deeply, pretending to get a whiff of a pie cooling on the kitchen counter.

She slowed down as if to take in every sight and sound Watson Lane held that day. *It's the end of an era.* Three children were playing basketball, and two more were riding bikes. A young man was loading up his boat with an ice chest and fishing gear. A young mother was pushing a toddler in a fancy stroller with cup holders, and an older woman walked briskly down the street with her back to Kaitlyn.

Grandma's neighbors . . . I wonder if they know. Some of them probably do. Others may be surprised when the For Sale sign goes up.

The left turn into the driveway nearly took her breath away. She suddenly realized how unprepared she was for this moment. Her grandmother's house without her grandmother. It just didn't seem right.

Even though Grandma had been sick for five years, Grandpa had always taken care of her. Now the disease had progressed, and he was tired. He had called Kaitlyn's mother and said he was ready to move in with her and to put Grandma in a nursing home. It would be better, they all agreed. None of the family lived in Natchitoches, and it was hard for Kaitlyn's mom to check on her elderly parents. With the move back to Alexandria, they would all be able to see each other more often. Today was moving day.

Kaitlyn put the car in park, closed her eyes, and said a prayer for her family as they bid farewell to a house and a life they loved. She walked to the front door, trying to avoid stepping on the pecans that dotted her path. She glanced toward the carport, half expecting the fish fryer to be sending up steam. It wasn't.

The screen door squeaked and squawked as she opened it.

"Well, there you are, honey," her grandpa said from his favorite chair.

Kaitlyn smiled at him, always amazed at how he had stayed the same sweet man in spite of the difficult years of caring for a wife with Alzheimer's. "Hi, Grandpa. How's Grandma doing?"

"She's about the same. She's in her bed." He grew a little somber. "Kaity, she may not recognize you this time, but remember she loves you just the same."

"I know, Gramps. I'll never forget that." Kaitlyn swallowed the lump in her throat and hugged him tightly. "I can't wait to see her. Where's Mom and Dad?"

"Packing up the bedroom. Your mother sent me out here to take a break."

Kaitlyn wished the hallway could be as long as it had seemed when she was younger, but instead it felt shorter than ever. In just a few steps she could see her grandmother staring out the window.

"Hi, Grandma!" She tried to sound cheerful. Her grandmother turned her head as if she was ready to acknowledge the person speaking, but no words came. Kaitlyn sat on the bed beside her.

"Grandma, it's Kaity." She took her grandmother's hand and started the one-sided conversation. "I just got here. It was a beautiful drive over this morning." Searching for words, she added, "Are you looking at those nice pecan trees in the yard?" Kaitlyn watched as her grandma tried unsuccessfully to fit the pieces together. Finally, with a wrinkled brow and a faraway look, her grandmother managed a weak "Hello." It was all Kaitlyn could do to not break down and cry.

"Kaitlyn," her mother called from the guest bedroom. "Come on in here. We have so much to show you."

Kaitlyn kissed her grandma on the forehead and said she'd be right back. She crossed the hall and found her mom and dad knee-deep in memorabilia. School pictures, coloring pages from Sunday-school lessons, old letters, and an assortment of homemade crafts covered the bed and much of the floor.

"Hey, Mom and Dad," Kaitlyn said as she hugged both her parents. "Mom, it's too hard. How are you getting through this?" She picked up a photo of herself and Grandma with their Easter bonnets on. She just stared at the photo, unable to speak further.

"Kaitlyn, it is hard. You're right. We're so caught up in the memories, we can hardly pack. But we're making a little progress. I wanted you to see these things in case we don't unpack them for a while. Someone else in our family needs to know what treasures will be stored in these plastic bins." Kaitlyn was impressed at how neatly her mom was preserving the family mementos.

Her grandfather joined them and surveyed the room with a sweet but heavy sigh. "Kaity, your grandmother loved you kids so much. Just look around this room and you'll see that she always wanted you near her. If she couldn't be at a school play or ball game, she'd have your mother save some item for her so she could feel as though she'd been there. When she got to go, she always brought something back to remind her of the good time she had.

"But she also left something for you. A few years ago, before her memory got too bad, she wrote each of you kids a letter. I've saved them until now. Your grandma knew this time would come, but she was prepared." He handed a letter to Kaitlyn.

Her hands shook as she opened it, and she had to wipe tears from her eyes in order to make out the writing.

Dear Kaity,

I remember standing outside the hospital nursery, watching you wiggle your mouth to form that same dimple your mother has. I think your grandpa had to pry me away after an hour of just staring at you. From that first moment on, I have never been disappointed in you. You have brought nothing but joy to my life.

I know you're sad that I'm not with you as I used to be. But dearest Kaity, while I may be silent on the outside, inside I'm full of memories of you. Look in every drawer and every closet of this house and you'll see evidence of the memories I've tucked away.

I know you're there taking care of me and your grandpa, and I want to thank you for loving us and allowing us to share your life. One more thing— look in the kitchen drawer beside the telephone and get that recipe for pecan pie. I know you can make them just as good as mine!

I love you forever,
Grandma

Tears spilled down Kaitlyn's cheeks as she dissolved into her mother's comforting embrace. Soon they were all holding on to each other in the tiny bedroom on Watson Lane.

"Well," Grandpa said, clearing his throat. "I'm hungry."

Kaitlyn looked down at the letter she still held. "Grandpa, let's go find that recipe. What this house needs is the smell of a fresh pecan pie."

Continuing
the Legacy

Chapter Seven

Let My love compel you. Living a legacy of love is the excellent way! Share with others what they need. Let My statutes be your heritage and the joy of your heart. As you live every day, set your heart on following My instructions.

Blessing you,
Your Creator

—from 2 Corinthians 5:14; 1 Corinthians 13:13;
Romans 12:13; Psalm 119:111–112

You sit beside them on a riverbank, sharing a fishing pole. You stand on a stool beside them, patting down biscuit dough. You lounge on the back porch with them as you watch frogs play on a hot summer day. You think you're just having a fun day. But what you don't realize is how much joy you're bringing to some of the people who love you most—your grandparents.

Watching a granddaughter laugh and play is one of a grandparent's favorite pastimes. But sharing with her the many valuable lessons we've gained throughout our lives ranks among the most rewarding activities too. Some people say God gave us grandchildren so we could make up for everything we forgot to teach our own children. But that's not really true. It's just that we love you so much we want to do everything we can to equip, inspire, and encourage you to thrive, to make a difference, to leave a legacy.

So thank you for your patience when we seem determined to teach you everything we know. Thanks for spending time with us and for letting us share our hearts with you. For being our best legacy. We couldn't be more proud.

One thing, and only one,
in this world has eternity
stamped upon it. Feelings
pass; opinions change.
What you have done lasts—
lasts in you. Through
ages, through eternity,
what you have done
for Christ, that, and
only that, you are.

◆

F. W. Robertson

"It smells funny. Why do I have to go?" Alicia had pleaded as a child. Now she was glad she'd gone.

cookie day

The smell of freshly baked cookies filled the kitchen as Alicia looked under the table for her daughter's missing shoe. "Come on, sweetie," she yelled from an upside-down position, grabbing the missing shoe with one hand and balancing herself with the other. "The cookies are almost ready. You know how Granny looks forward to this day and will be waiting for us."

She looked up just as five-year-old Amy came running into the kitchen with an armload of dolls. "Mommy, can I take my new Barbies to show Granny? She might want to play with them." The energetic youngster, one shoe on and one shoe off, was peeking through blond and brunette Barbie dolls—two dressed in fancy gowns and two more in the latest sports clothes.

"Sure. Granny will love to see your dolls. Let's get your shoe on, then you can put your dolls in your backpack." Alicia reached down to pick up Amy and set her on the kitchen table, at a more adult-friendly shoe-tying height. "I'll put the cookies in a plastic box. Then we'll be ready to go."

Amy jumped down and ran to the back of the house, pigtails bouncing. Alicia smiled as she thought of how much joy Amy had brought to Granny.

Her grandmother had only been in the nursing home for three months. She was adjusting well, but Alicia knew how important the visits from family and friends were to her. It was her grandmother who had taught her the Biblical principle of caring for those who are "shut in."

It's still hard to believe these trips are now to visit my grandmother instead of going with her to visit others, Alicia thought as she scooped cookies into a plastic container. She shook her head in lingering disbelief. *The same nursing home where she's spent years ministering to the occupants . . . I should be picking her up to go with me, not going to see her there.*

Alicia had only been two years old when her grandmother started including her in her shut-in ministry. Once a week they would bake cookies and head to the nursing home to encourage the patients who lived there. It was clear to Alicia even then that the senior citizens loved seeing someone young, and for many years she loved being the center of attention. But as she got older, Alicia had found the trips less pleasant and had begged her mother to let her stay home.

"Mom, it smells funny. Why do I have to go?" she would plead. *So much complaining about doing such a simple act of kindness*, she thought now.

"Honey, it's so important to your grandmother," her mom had answered. "You'll be glad once you go." That hadn't always been true then, but now she was glad she had gone. She cherished the heritage of love her grandmother had handed down to her and was grateful for the opportunity to hand that down to her own daughter.

"Mommy, I'm ready." Amy pulled at Alicia's jeans, trying to get her attention.

Alicia patted her on the head. "I am too. Let's go."

Once they were on their way, Amy began her usual chattering and asking questions. "Mommy, why does Granny live with all those other people?"

"Remember, I told you Granny is a little sick now, and your Grandma Parker can't take care of her anymore. She needs a nurse to take care of her." Alicia thought of her mother's struggle as she had made the difficult decision to put her own mother in a nursing home.

"Oh, I forgot." Amy seemed satisfied with that simple explanation. Alicia looked in the rearview mirror to see her daughter's contented face. She glanced up at herself in the mirror and noticed that she didn't look quite as peaceful. But she knew the truth—that her grandmother was sicker than "a little." Her chronic lung disease had progressed so that she suffered from frequent bouts of pneumonia. It was a condition she had lived with for years, but at eighty-eight years old, her body was tiring of the fight.

"Mommy, tell me about when you were little and would go to the nursing home with Granny." Amy had asked to hear the familiar story over and over again.

"OK, but you've heard this story so many times. Aren't you tired of it?"

"Nope," Amy responded from the backseat.

"Well, when I was little, every Tuesday morning at 9:45, Granny would pick me up to go to the nursing home with her. She always brought homemade cookies, carefully stacked in a shoe box, for me to pass out to her friends. I would hold the box on my lap as we drove and try to not eat them all before we got there." Alicia let out a little giggle at the memory. "Of course, I couldn't resist at least one. And Granny would make sure she had enough so I could eat one on the way. It was always the same kind of cookie—a tea cake. She said her friends didn't need a lot of sugar, and those didn't have much sugar in them."

"Did they like that kind?"

"You bet. It's the same kind we make when we have time—like we did this morning." Alicia picked up the story again. "In those days, kids didn't have to sit in car safety seats, so I sat right next to Granny. If she had to stop quickly, she'd reach over really fast and hold me back with her arm." She added softly, almost to herself, "I always felt safe with Granny."

Alicia smiled and could almost feel the comfort of snuggling next to her grandmother. "We would sing all the way to the nursing home. 'Jesus Loves Me' and 'Victory in Jesus' were our favorites. Once we got there, Granny would open the door and waltz in like she was famous, and her friends would be waiting for her. Some were in wheelchairs, some were in beds in their rooms, some would be watching TV on the couches. But they all knew who she was and were happy to see her."

"Just like when we go. Right, Mommy?"

Alicia looked again in the mirror to see her daughter grinning. "Just like when we go," she affirmed with a smile. "You know, it makes Granny very happy that we're continuing what she started."

Amy didn't respond, and Alicia glanced back to see a concerned look on her daughter's face.

"Mommy, who will do this when I go to kindergarten?" School would be starting in two weeks.

"You know, I've been thinking about that. When I

was little, Granny went every Tuesday morning—I only went with her in the summer. But since Granny is there now, maybe we could change our cookie day to Tuesday afternoon, after school. How does that sound?"

"I like that idea," Amy responded. "I don't want to stop seeing Granny."

Soon Alicia and Amy arrived at Plantation Manor. Armed with a box of cookies and a backpack full of Barbies, the cookie team swung open the door, ready to make someone's day brighter. Alicia looked around for her grandmother, but she wasn't in her usual waiting spot in the foyer. Alicia approached the nurse's station, trying not to sound alarmed, in spite of the sudden knot in her stomach. "Good morning," she said, "I didn't see my grandmother, Mrs. Hacker. Do you know if she's in her room?"

The nurse looked down at Amy and back at Alicia. The deliberate eye contact was all Alicia needed to tell her things were not right.

"Good morning, Alicia."

Alicia could tell the thoughtful nurse was keeping her tone light to protect Amy.

"We called you and your mother, but you had apparently already left. Your grandmother had a bit of a rough night. She's running a little fever, and the doctor would like to put her in the hospital."

Alicia took a deep breath as she absorbed this new information.

"Mommy, let's go see Granny." Amy was tugging at Alicia's leg again, not comprehending the reason for delay. "She's probably waiting for us to pass out our cookies."

Alicia spoke again to the nurse, asking more with her eyes than she could with her words. "Should we go on in to see her?"

"I think so," the nurse responded. "She's just resting until the ambulance comes to take her to the hospital."

Amy squatted down to meet her eager daughter at eye level. "Amy, Granny's not feeling well today. She won't be able to walk around with us as we deliver the cookies. The doctor is going to take her to the hospital so she can get better and come back to help us. We can go see her, but we have to be a little quieter than usual. OK?"

"OK."

"OK, let's go." Alicia turned and headed toward her grandmother's room, but Amy took off in the opposite direction.

"Whoa, missy," Alicia gently grabbed her daughter's arm and tickled her stomach. "Granny's room is this way."

"But what about the cookies? Everyone's waiting

for them and for us to go and make them smile."

Alicia caught her breath as she looked at her inno-cent but thoughtful daughter. *Just like Granny—she'd be so proud.* Her throat clenched as she tried to hold back emotions her little girl wouldn't yet understand. "You're right, Amy." She swallowed hard. "Let's pass some out on the way to Granny's room."

Amy giggled as she took the cookie box from her mom and headed toward an older woman in a wheel-chair. Alicia could barely hold back her tears as she watched a legacy in action. Amy opened the box, took out a cookie, and handed it to the woman. "Do you know Granny?" Alicia heard Amy say. "She lives here now. She taught my mommy how to make these cookies so we could bring you one. I hope you like it."

The woman's face brightened as she took the cookie and patted Amy on the head, and Alicia was taken back thirty years to the many times she'd had similar interactions. She remembered feeling the warmth of her grandmother's smile that communi-cated love and pride in her.

"See my backpack?" Alicia heard Amy tell her new friend. "My Barbies are in here. I'm going to leave one with Granny to keep her company when I have to go to school."

The wrinkled lady in the wheelchair had tears glis-tening in her eyes as she spoke softly to Amy. "I think your Granny will love to have a Barbie to keep her company. You are a very thoughtful granddaughter." She reached out to give Amy a hug. "Thank you for the cookie. You've made my day."

As Alicia watched Amy walk proudly back to her, she knew this was one tradition worth keeping.

Look for these other great Hugs™ books